FINDING GOD
IN LONELINESS

ANTONIO RITACCIO

All booklets are published
thanks to the generosity of the supporters
of the Catholic Truth Society

All Scriptural quotations in this booklet are from the Revised Standard Version (RSV). The abbreviation *'CCC'* followed by a number indicates a paragraph in the *Catechism of the Catholic Church*.

Image Credits
Page 4, © Jan Jenka/Shutterstock.com
Page 27, © Adam Jan Figel/Shutterstock.com
Page 44, © BsWei/Shutterstock.com
Page 58, © Renata Sedmakova/Shutterstock.com

All rights reserved. First published 2018 by The Incorporated Catholic Truth Society, 40-46 Harleyford Road, London SE11 5AY Tel: 020 7640 0042 Fax: 020 7640 0040. Copyright © 2018 The Incorporated Catholic Truth Society

ISBN 978 1 78469 565 1

Contents

You Are Not Alone!. 5

Hungry for a Word 17

When We Cannot Escape Loneliness 32

When We Can Do Something about Loneliness . . . 43

Praying in Loneliness 55

Prayers. 66

Useful Resources in the UK. 70

Bibliography. 72

You Are Not Alone!

Are you lonely? Feelings of loneliness can affect everyone – young mothers and their babies, the elderly and their carers, pupils and teachers, the police and criminals, soldiers and doctors, seafarers and truckers, clergy and lay people, the rich and famous as well as the poor and homeless. It is tempting to see the feeling of loneliness as a modern problem that needs to be fixed like a broken machine. Countless books have been written on the subject with advice on how to eradicate loneliness from our lives, but often without addressing the reason why we feel lonely in the first place. For some, the solution to coping with their loneliness is to rely on the constant supply of images and films on the internet and television. For others, it is to bury themselves in being busy, at the office or school, with agendas crammed with meetings and piles of paper precariously balanced over untidy desks. At least if they live in a world of paper-made chaos, they will never have time to be lonely. For still others, the lure of alcohol, drugs and pornography provides a temporary but lethal solution to loneliness. But the reality is that for all our distractions we are merely passing the time, and deep down we still feel dissatisfied. In moments of clarity, such as in the dead of night, we may wake up to recognise that sooner or later our time will run out, and we can begin to become anxious because we realise that our lonely lives have no meaning. Loneliness can call into question the very purpose of our existence by presenting us with a spirit of emptiness and nothingness so profound that we can find ourselves faced with the prospect that we are utterly alone in the Universe. In this darkness, we can be gripped by the terrifying realisation that we are ultimately homeless – we do not belong. If this is your experience, and you are living with an unshakable feeling of loneliness, then the Church invites you to take courage: God has not abandoned you; he wants to help you!

Who Am I?

In the face of our mortality, loneliness has become one of the most common subjects of art and literature because it points to the very question of our identity – "who am I?" This question affects everyone in every generation, yet very few people are willing to admit that they feel lonely because of the stigma attached. We tend to assume that if a person has no friends it is because they have been rejected by their peers, and no one wants to be labelled by others as a 'reject'. However, the feeling of loneliness, instead of crushing us, can become a significant mechanism that leads us to discover who we are when we look beyond ourselves for an answer to our identity. The Church proposes that if we search for an answer with humility, we will find it in the form of a God who created us. He is not some lonely God out there in an infinite universe, but instead, he is a God of love and relationship, who is just dying for you to know him.

Man, in the Image and Likeness of God

In the very first Chapter of the Bible, we find an account of the creation of the world. It is not the sort of explanation that you would expect to find in a science book. It was written instead to answer the question of why man exists rather than how he came to exist. Pope St John Paul II (1920-2005) teaches us that our loneliness is rooted in our frustrated need to be connected with God and with others. We were made for communion. We are called to know God and at the same time to find fulfilment in being in a relationship with others. Not only was man created by God – male and female – but unlike horses, trees, mountains and all other created things, he was created in God's image and likeness (cf. *Gn* 1:26). Only man can know himself as a person – a 'someone' and not a 'something' – only he can make moral choices to determine his future. Man, both male and female, enjoys a unique relationship of solitude with God. Only he can talk with God and experience communion with him. In the task of naming all the animals (*Gn* 2:19-20), he also discovers his hunger for communion with another person like himself (Pope John Paul II, *Meaning of Man's Original Solitude*, General Audience 10 October 1979). We see in the Book of Genesis how Adam is delighted to meet the woman, Eve, because he sees in her such a person. Adam discovers the full meaning of his existence in giving himself as an unconditional gift to Eve who, unlike the animals, has the capacity to receive him as a gift. Equally, he receives the generous gift that Eve makes of herself. They experience no shame at this stage because they experience each other as a union of persons, rather than as objects. The word solitude is sometimes used in a negative sense of being cut off from the world. That is what happens to prisoners who are put into solitary confinement as a form of punishment. Instead, Adam and Eve found a shared solitude in their union and so here the word solitude means undivided attention. We find fulfilment only in being present to another person with our whole being.

Man Loses Sight of His Identity

When man accepted the subtle lie of the Serpent in the Garden of Eden, he took as fact that God cannot be trusted, even though God's generosity was self-evident. Man rebelled against God and declared his own capacity to choose between good and evil as the truth (*Gn* 3:1-8).

This is a constant theme that we see in our lives today when we accept as truth the pernicious lies of the Ancient Serpent. He subtly whispers into our ears that we are victims, and so, outraged and offended, we declare a violent war on the world by our long, sad faces. Because of sin, man's original capacity for solitude is obscured by concupiscence, which the Catechism of the Catholic Church describes as: "lust of the flesh, lust of the eyes, and pride of life" (cf. *CCC* 2514). Man now finds himself a betrayer of his creator, and in this way he loses sight of his identity as a person created in the image and likeness of God. He is now terrified of God and hides from him. With the joy of communion now lost, he attempts to grasp for a meaning to his solitary existence apart from God, by using the world around him as a means of satisfying his need for intimacy and communion. However, without God as his point of reference – he now sees other people as 'things' which can be grasped at to satisfy his own desires rather than as persons to whom he can give his life to.

The key to understanding the account of the Fall is to find ourselves in Adam and Eve (*Gn* 3:1-19). Their experience is ours. It is tempting to now think of God in the Heavens looking disapprovingly down on humanity and shaking his head with disgust at our troubles. However, ultimately, we are all victims of the lies of the Devil who tells us that God cannot be trusted. We know what it is like to be separated from God, but we also recognise within us a desire for communion with each other and solitude with God. The rest of the Bible is a testament to how God has been fighting against our rebellious nature to win us back. The truth is that God is not our enemy; he loves us and is on our side. He is "merciful and gracious, slow to anger, and abounding in steadfast love and faithfulness" (*Ex* 34:6).

The Experience of Loneliness

Loneliness affects everyone at some stage in their life. We experience it in different ways. It is the experience of being disconnected. For some, it can be a mild and passing trial. For others, it seems to follow them around relentlessly like a heavy, sickening sensation in the pit of the stomach. Those of us who suffer from mental illness, such as depression or anxiety, can find it very difficult to explain what we are feeling or make ourselves understood. We can be embarrassed about trying to explain ourselves, and so we end up brushing off other people's concerns. We can find ourselves alone even though we may be surrounded by people who love and accept us. For some of us, having poor experiences with trusted friends can lead us to put up barriers to prevent ourselves from being hurt again. We can become emotionally distant with our friends, pushing them further away from us. Our experience of loneliness can lead us to deeper levels of depression. Loneliness can feel as if there is no escape.

We may think that we must change our behaviour to be accepted. However, for some of us, our loneliness is a call to change our circumstances, to challenge our thinking patterns, to humble ourselves and ask forgiveness from those we may have offended. If we have hurt the person we love, it is not surprising that we find ourselves alone. In this case, the cure for loneliness is to accept that we were wrong and to say sorry without reservation.

For others, our loneliness is a trial that cannot be changed. For example, in the case of sickness and death or homelessness. For some of us, the death of a beloved pet can be as devastating as losing a relative. The loneliness and pain of finding ourselves unable to express our loss to someone who understands us can be made worse if we feel we are being ridiculed for being overly sentimental. We may end up helplessly alone because we have been abandoned by our family in our old age, or because of life-changing experiences such as sickness, leaving our home behind, starting a new career or beginning our studies at university. We can feel isolated because we are misunderstood or we find it hard to understand others. These are the sorts of circumstances that we have little control over. In these trials, the Lord calls us to trust, to wait and to hope in his providence and to know that our trial will come to an end.

However, there are some instances where it is not so clear if we are called to change our circumstances, or to carry our burden with patience. In these cases the Holy Spirit makes us know the difference and how we should deal with our situation (cf. *CCC* 2847). He is given to us in Baptism and Confirmation as the Spirit of Adoption, uniting us to Christ (cf. *CCC* 690). To have friends, we need to be a friend. We can feel lonely because we are not very good at making friends. We can feel shy and perceive ourselves as being unworthy of others' attention, and so we may end up neglecting the friends we have. However, our shyness may be a result of pride. We can be fearful that others will think poorly of us, and so we can end up demonising them and the world as being against us. In this case, we need to humble ourselves and ask God for the gift of humility so that we are not concerned by what others think of us. If we are ashamed of ourselves because of our lack of education or social skills, we may need to renounce the idol of popularity and fame.

Believing the Lie That We Are Rejected

Our experience of rejection can bring us to feel chronically lonely. We may feel that nothing can satisfy our craving to be wanted and connected with others. In this case, we may be oppressed by a spirit of rejection. It may be, for example, that our mothers were plagued by the illness of depression after our birth, and they found it difficult to show us the love and attention that we needed. Perhaps there were long periods in our infancy when we were not picked up, held and cherished. Or possibly growing up we found ourselves at times rejected by our siblings or just abandoned and left alone. There may be an underlying feeling that we are not wanted. This perception can affect the way we relate to others daily. We may believe that there is something wrong with us, that we are unlovable and that nobody wants to spend time with us. This fear can paralyse us to the point of not being able to make friends quickly – the fear of rejection prevents us from accepting social engagements, and so we end up alone. The spirit of dejection may even cripple us to the extent that we can see no point in praying to God. The Church, however, calls us to turn away from every spirit of oppression by looking steadily at God's love for us. She invites us to renounce the lie that we are not loved or cherished. We are called to turn away from introspection and instead to look at what God, as our Heavenly Father, has revealed about himself. The truth is that God has created us because he wants us. He cherishes us and takes delight in us (*Zp* 3:17). From the moment of our conception, he rejoiced at our coming into existence (cf. *Jr* 1:5). He gave us a unique and eternal soul, and at the hour of our birth, he cried tears of delight. He is proud of us as the work of his hands – he made us in his own image and likeness (cf. *Is* 64:8). He applauded our first steps, and since then every achievement that we have made has been recorded and remembered.

God's Love as a Balm for Loneliness

If we search for God, we will find him; if we knock on his door, he promises to open it for us (cf. *Mt* 7:7-8). To find God in loneliness is to discover medicine for our wound. Ultimately, everything we do is really a search to recover our lost solitude with God. The problem with our fallen human nature is that we can often miss the mark, and in our search, we tend to get blown off course and end up giving ourselves to created things in a harmful way – alcohol, food, sex, money, fame, power, etc. These are some of the idols that we give our lives to in the false belief that they will, in turn, provide us with life. Attraction to these destructive idols can become addictions that render us isolated and chronically lonely. Throwing ourselves into our work and being extremely busy can also be a way of trying to address loneliness. Somehow, overly busy people tend not to be very productive. But running around, trying to fix things and making everything they do into a complicated farce can be a subtle way of camouflaging the unbearable realisation that if they stop to listen to their inner silence for even just a moment, they will be sickened by the emptiness they find. Silence with God is solitude; without him it is loneliness. If we are to discover God as a balm for our loneliness, we need to renounce the idols of this world and all the distractions that claim our attention daily. We must face up to the possibility that God will only enter our loneliness if we give him permission to enter. For this reason, we need to find moments where we can allow God to be alone with us, in a lonely place. Our Lord describes it as our 'private room' where we can be alone in prayer with God as our Heavenly Father (*Mt* 6:6). Perhaps you have suffered from long periods of loneliness all your life. Perhaps you have found yourself crying bitterly, alone on your bed at night, desperately longing for your pain to end. In your torment, the Lord has heard your cry. To the invisible plight of your loneliness, God is not indifferent. He wants to set you free and to be a sign to others of his intimate love for each one of us. The Church's proclamation of the Good News is an invitation to discover the healing medicine of the God of relationship. He wants to enter into communion with you. The Church invites you to make the prayer of the Apostle Philip your own: "Lord, show us the Father, and we shall be satisfied" (*Jn* 14:8).

Prayer

O Lord, I sometimes feel alone by myself. I am sorry that I have not always trusted in your promises. Thank you for sharing your Divine life with me. Please help me to recognise when I am hiding from you and grant me the joy of being alone with you instead, through Christ our Lord. Amen.

Tips for Finding God in Loneliness

- By admitting to ourselves that we are lonely, we can begin to allow ourselves to take responsibility and begin to address our needs.

- Try using the acronym HALT devised by Alcoholics Anonymous. Stop what you are doing and address your need when you feel HUNGRY, ANGRY, LONELY or TIRED. Remember, for example, that being hungry can mean hunger for friendship as well as food.

- Meditate on God's promise in Scripture that he knows you "I have called you by name, you are mine." Read Isaiah 43:1-5.

Hungry for a Word

Would you like never to feel lonely again? Loneliness can be compared to the pangs of hunger and thirst. The rumblings in our stomachs and the dryness in our throats are not problems to be eradicated, but safety mechanisms that warn us when we need to eat and drink; otherwise, we would not survive. Our hunger and thirst are not like an annoying and useless car alarm that keeps going off for no reason – we disable those. Our bodies use these warning signs to tell us when something needs to be addressed. Our human nature has been wounded by Original Sin, and so it tends towards concupiscence. If we did not experience loneliness, we would end up becoming totally self-absorbed with our own problems. To a large extent, that is the definition of hell. No, we address the pangs of hunger and thirst with a plate of food and a glass of water. Similarly, the feeling of loneliness reminds us that it is not good for us to be alone (cf. *Gn* 2:18).

Resting with God

Taking time to rest is necessary for us to operate normally. Otherwise, we risk exhaustion. We can become tired of being with others and weary of being alone. However, our rest finds its correct place in the Third Commandment – Remember to keep holy the Lord's Day – where we find our true respite by placing ourselves in the presence of God (cf. *CCC* 2168ff). When we thirst for God, we discover him to be like refreshing water (cf. *Is* 55:1). The idea of a self-indulgent 'me-time' has become very popular these days, where the idea of resting is not so much to be refreshed, but rather to take a 'holiday' from our relationship with God and from our concern for others – we just want to be left alone. In the end, however, we end up becoming more tired with life. St Paul tells us that it is in Christ's love that we find new satisfying energy and power that urges us to live for others.

> For the love of Christ urges us on, because we are convinced that one has died for all; therefore, all have died. And he died for all, that those who live might live no longer for themselves but for him who for their sake died and was raised. (*2 Co* 5:14-21)

The Word of God Is Food for Our Souls

Everyone needs to be loved and cherished. We need friends to speak and laugh with. Many of us who live alone yearn to feel that we belong to someone. The UK social network campaign called Campaign to End Loneliness issued a report in 2017 stating that chronic loneliness can seriously affect our health in the same way as smoking fifteen cigarettes a day (*www.campaigntoendloneliness.org*). This fact has long been known. The psychoanalyst, René Árpád Spitz (1887-1974), released a documentary film based on his research into the high mortality rate of infants in orphanages. The film, entitled *Psychogenic Disease in Infancy* (1952), concludes that one in three babies were dying because of a lack of affection. Those who survived showed signs of long-term and significant mental and physical health issues. Spitz blamed these problems on the children's lack of a personal relationship with a caring adult: no one ever played peek-a-boo with these babies, or held them when they cried. These children were literally starved of the food of love. We grow and flourish when our identities are fed by others, in the way in which we interact with them. At a deep level, we too can find ourselves hungering to be wanted and cherished.

At the baptism of Jesus in the Jordan, Jesus was fully conscious of his identity as the Beloved (*Mt* 3:13-17). His relationship with his Heavenly Father was food that not even his disciples knew about (*Jn* 4:32). It sustained him during his fast for forty days in the loneliness of the wilderness and in the face of every temptation by Satan to doubt his identity as the Son of God (*Mt* 4:1-11).

In the desert of our own loneliness, we too will often hear the voice of the Tempter. In the desert of old age, we can be alone and defenceless, and likewise when we are sick, and when we feel rejected and abandoned. In these moments of hunger for love, the consoling words of the Father can become our food – we too are the beloved children of God, we too are cherished, held and loved by the Lord in his embrace.

The Food of Communion

Increasingly, people are finding themselves anonymous and alone in our towns and cities. A significant cause of loneliness in our world today is a growing crisis in family life. Children can find themselves with fewer siblings and unable to support their parents alone in old age. Many of us are witnessing the breakdown of marriages around us and an increasing disregard for marriage as a public obligation. In many cases it seems easier for couples to cohabit, but this arrangement does not give them the social boundaries they need to work at their relationship when friction appears. In the end it is women, the young and the elderly who find themselves abandoned and suffering the most (cf. Pope Francis, *Address to Participants in the International Colloquium*, 17 November 2014). We all need to feel that we belong to someone and that we are wanted. The Church can provide an antidote to this kind of loneliness.

Small Christian prayer or social groups can play an important role in supporting us in our family lives and helping us to connect with others in the wider parish community, since we can often find ourselves lost in the larger assemblies at Mass on Sundays. The goal of a Christian community is to live out Christ's command to love one another as he loved us (*Jn* 13:34). However, our experience of community life is not always positive. As we grow in familiarity, there is always a chance that we can be put off from remaining in these groups as judgements and arguments can begin to surface between us. Conflicts are a very normal part of every community experience, including family life. We should not panic when arguments appear; they are opportunities for us to cultivate a spirit of truth and to lean on the Lord for communion. In this way, our honest and sometimes hurtful discussions can be transformed into moments of growth. The people we get to know especially well can be very good at pointing out our flaws and defects, but they can also help us to grow in love and unity when we remain Christ-centred. The Sacrament of Confession is especially important in cultivating the habit of remaining rooted in a life of grace. We must learn how to eat the food of humility and to ask for forgiveness.

It was for this reason that Jesus sent out his disciples in pairs. Two is the smallest number of people that is needed for communion to be made visible. Being part of a pair helped them against the sin of pride as they would inevitably end up disagreeing at times about where they were to go, what they were to eat and so on. They had to learn to love one another. The disciples were commanded to forgive each other constantly (*Mt* 18:21). When we are single and live alone, we run the risk of never discovering that we might be proud and disagreeable people. If we have never been confronted by another, we may believe that we are saintly and end up judging those around us who argue and fight all the time. Perhaps we can be scandalised by the arguments and fights that break out in our families and communities. Mindful of the scourge of divorce, which is so prevalent and accepted in our society, when couples row it is tempting for them to think that they are no longer compatible with each other. They may begin to think that their marriage was a mistake, and so they are tempted to separate as everyone else is doing. When strong differences of opinion surface in our communities and hidden judgements begin to invade our opinions of one another, we may be tempted just to walk away. We might end up preferring to stay alone, eating the bread of solitude so as not to be disturbed – but as with families, we are called to speak the truth and to seek reconciliation with one another. Our failure to fulfil Christ's command to love one another as he has loved us only comes about when we fail to focus on the Word of God and the Eucharist as our food (*Jn* 15:7).

The Food of Love Alone

There is a traditional Christmas Eve custom in Poland of sharing a type of bread called *opłatek*. It is made to be shared between friends and to remind us of the communion we receive at Mass. It is especially comforting for single people who live alone to receive this bread as a sign that they are cherished and loved. For some of us, the hardest condition to accept is to remain single, unmarried and without a family of our own. As we find ourselves eating, sleeping and pottering about our homes alone, a spirit of comparison can begin to preoccupy us, where we compare ourselves to our friends who are already married and having children. Our hearts can sink when we see before us a life of loneliness. With each passing birthday, a spirit of panic can take hold of us as we begin to believe that we will never be married. However, this fear and panic is based on a lie that marriage is the solution to our loneliness. If that is the case, then we have made an idol out of our idea of being married. Many couples find themselves trapped in lonely and loveless marriages. Behind our anxiety to get married is perhaps a fear that we might remain alone, labelled unwanted and unlovable for the rest of our lives. However, it is simply not true that our happiness depends on not remaining single. Whether we get married or not, unless we are rooted in a relationship with God, we will never be truly happy. We are, each of us, called to accept God's invitation to discover him as the food for our souls and the fulfilment of our deepest longings. Whether we are married, single, a priest or religious, when we experience solitude with God, we find ourselves in a safe and secure place. We discover that we are wanted and cherished by God as our Heavenly Father. We can then begin to risk giving ourselves as food for others, as Christ gave himself for us. By giving the Lord our undivided attention, our state of life takes on its proper place as a calling to serve and an expression of our primary vocation to love.

The words "it is not good for man to be alone" (*Gn* 2:18) find their meaning not in seeing others as people who can take away our loneliness but rather in recognising that we are called to give ourselves to others. Husbands and wives are called to find the meaning of their vocation to love in giving themselves to each other in mutual support. Christians who find themselves single are called to find the expression of their vocation to love in the service of the Church community in offering hospitality, in caring for the sick and elderly of the parish, in supporting the evangelising mission of the Church through catechesis and teaching and so on. Since they do not have a family to look after they can offer to share with others the 'food' of their time in a way that married couples cannot. Accepting the call to serve the Church community as a single person does not exclude the possibility of finding a spouse to marry; however, those who are reconciled with their state of remaining single, either through circumstances or through choice, discover a new freedom. They fulfil their vocation to love by choosing to remain celibate and chaste, to lead a life of prayer and to offer their services to their parish community, while continuing to work in the world.

The Food of the Kingdom of God

Consecrated celibacy is a call to witness the Kingdom of God through the public renunciation of married life and the possibility of creating a family. To some, it may seem absurd in this day and age that there should be anyone without a sexual partner. But consecration to the celibate life is not a call to become sexually frustrated. It is rather a vocation to the undivided and chaste gift of self to everyone in service of the Church's mission. It is an anticipation of how we will relate to each other in the new Kingdom of God at the end of time (*Mt* 22:30). However, the pain of loneliness for those who live alone is inevitable. After interacting with people all day, celibates must retire to their rooms in solitude. However, far from being a terrible moment of suffering, the pangs of loneliness are a call to transform their hunger for companionship into solitude with the Lord – to find intimacy with God. When we search for him in our lonely places, God changes our loneliness into solitude with him. Celibate people are called to find the nourishment that sustains their life of service in an ever-deepening life of prayer.

The Food of Priestly Celibacy

Celibate people often feel lonely even though they can sometimes be in contact with lots of people every day. Ordained priests are icons of Christ. On the day of their ordination, they are set aside and consecrated to divide themselves amongst many, like the five loaves and two fish that Jesus shared with the five thousand on the other side of the Sea of Galilee (*Jn* 6:1-14). However, when a priest is low on energy and bereft of intimacy he can feel that everyone wants a 'piece' of him, especially when the miracle of multiplication is not happening, and he becomes fragmented instead! However, for a priest to be available to others in the same way that Jesus was in his earthly ministry, he needs to find solitude with the Lord. Jesus often went off to a lonely place to be alone with his Heavenly Father in prayer (*Lk* 5:16). He would spend the entire night praying (*Lk* 6:12). The other analogy of the priest as bread broken-and-shared is Christ's Body as the Bread of Life, given up for us in the Eucharist, in which we are also present at his Sacrifice on the Cross (*Lk* 22:19). Priests are often tempted to forget the stillness of this Cross where Jesus 'rested' and instead can find themselves overly busy. It can be a sign that they are struggling to pray. To accept Christ's invitation to let go of the daily distractions of parish work and to rest with him in that lonely place for a while is in a sense to risk 'free-falling' through the dark shadow

of loneliness and to trust that he is waiting there at the bottom to catch us (*Mk* 6:31). There always exists in priests a potential to not be accountable to anyone. They can end up staying up late, eating poorly, taking no exercise and praying only occasionally. Taking time to cultivate good priestly friendships and the company of faithfully married couples can be an antidote to this temptation. Priests tend to relax in the company of brother priests. It is also a blessing when they can pop in and rest for a bit with families, where they are treated as a brother rather than as a 'professional' holy man. There will always be work to do, and free time will never make itself available – it needs to be taken. Sometimes, the most surprising thing for priests is to discover that their parishes continue to function when they go on holiday.

Food for Discouragement in Pastoral Ministry

Any of us working in full-time pastoral ministry can become discouraged by our work when we see little fruit. Losing sight of why we are working in any given pastoral environment can put us in a lonely place, and we can be tempted to give up or become cynical. Bishops, priests, deacons, religious sisters, lay catechists, pastoral coordinators, and parish administrators, and also chaplains in prisons, schools and hospitals often find themselves working alone with little reward. If we are to flourish in our vocations, we need to find our consolation by receiving, and sharing daily, the proclamation of the Good News. In many cases, the people we minister to can appear half-hearted towards the treasures of the Church being made available to them. In the face of discouragement, the Kerygma – that is, the power of the Gospel message announced and received, with its call to repentance and faith – is the daily food of the apostolic life. Our zeal for souls is rekindled by the proclamation of the Good News, and the hearts of the people we minister to are stirred to discipleship when they hear it announced. The Kerygma declares that God has not abandoned us to the loneliness of our suffering and sins – he sent his only Son to save us. By his Cross and Resurrection the Lord has destroyed the works and lies of the Devil, and he is yearning for us to accept the gift of his free and unconditional love for us right now! We are invited to not look at our sins and weaknesses anymore but look towards heaven where we can discover God the Father who claims us as his beloved.

The Kerygma must be announced and received for it to give us life. The faith that it produces in us must also be sustained and fanned into a flame through prayer (*2 Tm* 1:6). The idea of taking time out to pray can sometimes seem impossible in our busy apostolate, but by committing to a living relationship with God we discover that our ministry seems to work better. The words of the psalm ring true here: "unless the Lord builds the house, those who build it labour in vain" (*Ps* 127:1a). The daily recitation of the Divine Office, which contains significant parts of Scripture and dogma, is the foundation of prayer for all priests, religious and some tertiary orders. However, even those who are not bound to pray it can find a great help in at least reciting some parts of the Office, such as morning and evening prayer. Regular Eucharistic Adoration, the daily Rosary and the prayerful reading of Scripture are priceless devotions that can help to galvanise the graces we receive at Mass. Regular retreats can help us to stay focused on what is essential in our ministry. We will also find a sure help in regular confession and spiritual direction. A rule of life is perhaps the most helpful tool in the apostolic life, by which we are gently held accountable by friends or a spiritual director for our vocation. This is particularly true for ordained ministers. A rule of life can be a simple set of 'rules' by which we aim to live our Christian life of prayer, service and our private and social life (Pope Paul VI, *Presbyterorum Ordinis*, 1965).

Prayer

Heavenly Lord, at times my loneliness overwhelms me, and I have no strength to carry on. Forgive me for the times I have failed to find rest in you and instead turned to distractions to feed me. I thank you for waiting for me and loving me in the Holy Eucharist. Please allow the fruit of the Good News to take root in my heart. Amen.

Tips for Finding God in Loneliness

- God is waiting to be discovered in others who are in need. Find ways to reach out to others who are lonely and in need. If you cannot leave the house, make a list of people that you know who would appreciate a phone call.

- Volunteer your time in visiting others who live alone. Ask your parish priest if he can arrange for you to visit or call someone who would like some company.

- Meditate on Christ's Judgement of the Nations. "Truly, I say to you, as you did it to one of the least of these my brethren, you did it to me" (*Mt* 31-46).

When We Cannot Escape Loneliness

The pangs of loneliness that surface in our hearts are a call to find a friend to connect with. However, this may not always be possible, especially when we become sick, or in advanced old age. Remaining single, becoming a widower and falling out of communion in marriage can also lead us to experience a loneliness that we cannot escape from. Some of us may be socially awkward, or we may find it hard to understand others, and so we can experience difficulties in making friends. Shyness and the fear of rejection can also be a huge stumbling block for us. We can become paralysed by the fear of rejection, and so we must endure loneliness alone. In all our trials the Church calls us to take courage because Jesus Christ knows our pain and comes to the aid of those who call on him (*CCC* 1880).

Loneliness in Old Age

As we get older, our social networks naturally tend to shrink because our friends pass away. For many, the loneliness of old age brings with it the trials of faith and the temptation to doubt God's Mercy and to fear what will become of us. However, the Church calls us to strengthen our resolve in the face of all our trials by keeping in mind that the Lord does not abandon us in our old age. There is a tender moment in the Gospel of John that can shed light on the question of the loneliness that often accompanies old age. After his resurrection, Jesus commissioned Peter to feed his flock. He then declared to him:

> Truly, truly, I say to you, when you were young, you fastened your own belt and walked where you would; but when you are old, you will stretch out your hands, and another will fasten your belt for you and carry you where you do not wish to go. (*Jn* 21:18)

Old age often brings with it the loss of freedom that we once enjoyed. Our bodies become slower, and we tend to feel chronic aches and pains; our eyesight becomes dimmer, and our hearing becomes harder. It is not so easy, under these circumstances, to go out and socialise. We may have to rely on our adult children to come and visit us, or if we have no family, we may find ourselves looking forward to a visit from a carer, a nurse or even a delivery person knocking on our door occasionally for the company. Many of us may be at the point where we cannot walk unaided, and we have to rely on others for everything, including 'tying up our belts'. Decisions about where we are to live, what we are to eat and what pills we must take can be taken out of our hands, and we may end up in places where we do not want to be. When Jesus spoke to Peter about his future, he was, in fact, talking about his death as a martyr. He wanted Peter to be ready. At the same time, we too are called to be ready to live out our old age as a type of martyrdom. By trusting in the providence of God, our periods of loneliness can be transformed from meaningless suffering to times of preparation for the Kingdom of God. Jesus admonishes us that we must become like little children to enter the Kingdom of God (*Mt* 18:3). We are called to give up our riches which are all the abilities that we have come to take for granted – our ability to communicate, to remember and to be coherent in our speech, to put on our own stockings and to walk to a neighbour's house (*Lk* 14:33). These are the treasures that many of us would not usually wish to give up by choice. Without them, we remain vulnerable and isolated. However, when we patiently hand over all our disabilities to the Lord as an offering of love, they become a testament that we are not made to live here forever, but for Eternal Life.

The elderly are sometimes portrayed in films as stereotypically decrepit, senile and comical. This kind of labelling undermines the true dignity of those who are old. The elderly have a noble mission of bridging the past with the future and handing onto future generations their wisdom and experience of life. Above all, the elderly are called to show the young how to grow old, to deal with sickness, old age and eventually death. Those of us who are raised without elderly grandparents are deprived of this invaluable education, and so without their example, we will find ourselves in unchartered waters when we grow old. In advanced old age and sickness, the elderly may especially be tempted to feel that they are not wanted because they may see themselves as a useless burden. We tend to link usefulness and independence with being valuable in our society, and so it is understandable that we might have such a low opinion of ourselves when we are needy. When we tell others that we do not want to be a burden to them, we may really be expressing a belief that we are of no value anymore. It is true that our needs in sickness and old age are not negligible; however, when we think about all those who came to the aid of Jesus in his hour of need, we can understand the value of our suffering in sickness and old age for those who take care of us.

When We Feel Abandoned

It may not be easy to accept help from others when we are used to being independent. Being left without help when we are in need can bring a crushing experience of loneliness. We may worry that we are being a nuisance. However, Jesus identifies with us in our weakness. Anyone who has visited the Marian Shrine of Lourdes in

France will have seen the way in which the sick visitors are treated – with priority. They are often carried as if they were Jesus himself. On his way to crucifixion, Jesus carried his heavy load alone. We can imagine his gratitude towards Simon of Cyrene who helped him. But it was Simon who benefitted more as the companion of Jesus (*Mk* 15:21). There was Veronica too. Tradition tells us that she managed to wipe the sweat and blood off his face with her veil. It was an act of kindness that gave our Lord some relief, but it was Veronica who was left with the more significant gift. Jesus left her with the image of his face imprinted on the cloth in his blood. In his final hour on the Cross, several women including his mother Mary stood nearby, supporting Jesus in his agony (*Jn* 19:25-27). His disciple John was there too. He did not abandon Jesus like the other disciples (*Mk* 14:50). We can imagine that his presence gave Jesus immeasurable consolation. But it was John who received the higher consolation as he heard his Master pronounce the words "John, behold your mother." This was not the story of some poor widow who was being taken care of in her old age. John became the son of the Queen of Heaven. She is known as the Glory of all the Saints, and now John was given the honour of becoming her son. In all these cases it was the one who was kind to Jesus that received the higher benefit. Even to this day, our Lord invites us to assist him so that we may receive the more significant benefit. Jesus identifies with the hungry, the thirsty, strangers and the naked, the sick and prisoners. He is with us in our need (*Mt* 25:35-36). This means that in our sickness and old age Jesus identifies with us so that those who support us receive the same gifts as those who cared for Jesus in his hour of need. If we refuse to accept help because we think we are too much of a burden, we are in fact denying them the chance to serve Jesus Christ crucified in us. It is an act of pride on our part, and we deny them the eternal rewards that God has prepared for them. If we have a genuine need, we must accept the help of others with humility. Similarly, when we are abandoned by those who have a care of duty for us in God's eyes, we must not give into the temptation to think that we are not worthy of care. Every person is made in the image and likeness of God (cf. *Gn* 1:26). We should instead intercede for them and ask the Lord to have Mercy on them so that we do not fall into the sin of bitterness. Those who neglect the needy will hear the words of condemnation from the Lord at the final judgement "where were you when I needed help?" (cf. *Mt* 25:41-46).

Loneliness from Fear

Fearing the judgements of others is not limited to sickness and old age. Some of us live with a deep-seated sense of unworthiness and low opinion of ourselves. This usually comes from past experiences of rejection, especially in our childhood. Our sense of worry about what people think of us can lead us to be suspicious of other people's motives, especially when they are kind towards us. We may believe an inner lie that something is wrong with us and that if we let our defences down, we will be exposed for others to see the 'real' us. Our fears can lead us to become hostile. Our fear is a call to daily repentance – to change the direction in which we are looking for security. At the heart of our isolation is the fear of rejection and loneliness. In our fear, we may find that we become people pleasers. We may need others to like us no matter what. Many of us have been drawn into terrible sins because we wanted others to like us. We can also end up clinging to others rather than giving them the freedom they need to like us freely. To move from loneliness to communion with others we must be able to take down our defences. It means, in a sense, giving others permission not to like us and to disagree with us. If we let go of our emotional demands that others must accept us, we will not be desolated if they reject us. As people pleasers we can become consumed by the very loneliness we were trying to avoid. We can end up unconsciously and unintentionally manipulating others to win their affection. This can lead to others avoiding us. No one is capable of really addressing our longings for communion if we are not free to be ourselves and to allow others the space they need because we limit our possibility for a genuine connection with them. Shyness can also be a painful source of suffering when we lack confidence in ourselves or are convinced that others will not like us. The fear of rejection, ridicule and humiliation can lead us to prefer to stay in the background. Shyness can cause us to be anxious about meeting people. It can make us feel self-conscious, so we can end up on our own and afraid behind closed doors. Shyness can be a trial which we are called to overcome through courage and humility. Jesus himself showed us the way through humility (*Ph* 2:6-7). Like Jesus, we are called to find ourselves by directing our affections towards God as our Heavenly Father. He knows and loves us as we are. He is the source of our communion.

Loneliness from Bereavement

For some, there are no words to express the loneliness that comes from the death of a loved one. In the days leading up to their passing, especially when they are in their final agony, we can be overwhelmed by grief as we gather around the person who is dying. For us also, when we are facing a terminal illness, we can have a deep sense of sadness and loneliness as we come to terms with the end of our life. In these moments our family and friends can provide us with invaluable help as we pass through these painful times. In the face of death Jesus tells us "let not your hearts be troubled, neither let them be afraid" (*Jn* 14:27). He gave us a 'way' beyond death which leads us to a new life in the Kingdom of God. This means that at the resurrection on the last day we will see each other again. Just before Jesus raised Lazarus from the dead, he brought his sister Martha to declare her faith in him:

> Jesus said to her, "Your brother will rise again." Martha said to him, "I know that he will rise again in the resurrection at the last day." Jesus said to her, "I am the resurrection and the life; he who believes in me, though he die, yet shall he live, and whoever lives and believes in me shall never die. Do you believe this?" She said to him, "Yes, Lord, I believe that you are the Messiah, the Son of God, the one coming into the world". (*Jn* 11:23-27)

These words can comfort us too because we know that Jesus does not abandon us to death. We can be confident that Jesus will raise us up again on the last day because he has already conquered death. His Apostles were eyewitnesses of his resurrection from the dead. They saw him ascending to heaven after he had promised that he would return to take them with him. From there he sends us the Holy Spirit as a pledge of his wonderful promise.

The Apostles saw all these things take place with their own eyes and have handed them onto us both in the living tradition of the Church and its Holy Scriptures. Jesus established the Church on his Apostles so that they could pass onto us the permanent memorial of his passion, death and resurrection through the Holy Sacrifice of the Mass.

In the face of our loss and loneliness, Christ himself assures us that whoever has faith in him will rise again from the dead in the Glory of God's Kingdom and the joy of Eternal Life (cf. *Jn* 11:26). We read in John's Gospel: "he who eats my flesh and drinks my blood has eternal life, and I will raise him up at the last day" (cf. *Jn* 6:54). The Mass makes present to us the saving events of Jesus's suffering and death on the Cross and his triumphant resurrection from the dead, and so we can be confident that through this same Sacrifice the Souls of the Faithful Departed are redeemed and justified before God. In the Mass, we are not alone because it makes present to us the entire Church, with all of the angels and the saints in heaven (*CCC* 1352). However, the Lord asks all of us who are his children to play our part in helping these suffering souls who are so grateful for our prayers. The funeral Mass is not a time for looking back with sadness but for looking forward with hope. By offering up the funeral Mass, we join the Kingdom of Heaven with all of the angels and saints at the Heavenly Banquet in asking our Heavenly Father for the most significant gift that can be given to our deceased loved ones: Mercy and Forgiveness. In the funeral Mass especially, we gather as the family of God to pray and sing the most beautiful prayer we possess. Through our worship of God and prayerful singing, we are united with all our departed brothers and sisters in heaven in praising God.

Prayer

Lord God, I know that you have made humanity in your own image and likeness, but I sometimes cannot help feeling worthless. I am so sorry that I have believed in the lie that I am not loveable and that I have closed myself off from you and from others. I thank you for entering my pain by dying on the Cross for me. Please renew in me your promise of Mercy and Eternal life. Amen.

Tips for Finding God in Loneliness

- We can feel compelled to make people like us if we fear being rejected by them. We need to let go of our false demands for happiness. Try to imagine yourself speaking to them and giving them permission to disagree with you or not to like you by saying: "I give you permission not to like me", or "I give you permission not to agree with me", etc.

- If you are housebound, make a list of people you wish to pray for and keep a regular appointment with yourself every day to bring them to the Lord in prayer.

- Meditate on the Lord's promises for your life in the Psalms: "O LORD, you have searched me and known me!" (*Ps* 139).

When We Can Do Something about Loneliness

If we believe that we are not needed by anyone our hearts can become hardened towards God and the world. We may find ourselves questioning whether our life is worth living. But the Church calls us to recognise the truth: that we are loved by God, and we are not alone. God never ceases to call us to be with him in our loneliness. By turning towards him in humility and in trust, we will find his company. By welcoming God's presence into our hearts, we can begin to discern how to take responsibility for our lives in the depth of our loneliness. For some of us, this means that we need to start taking steps towards changing our situation. For others, it means accepting our plight, trusting that our pain is part of God's plan to bring us to heaven by allowing us to identify with the suffering of Jesus. Our move towards God begins by welcoming the Good News. Pope Francis tells us that it is the answer to our negative experiences:

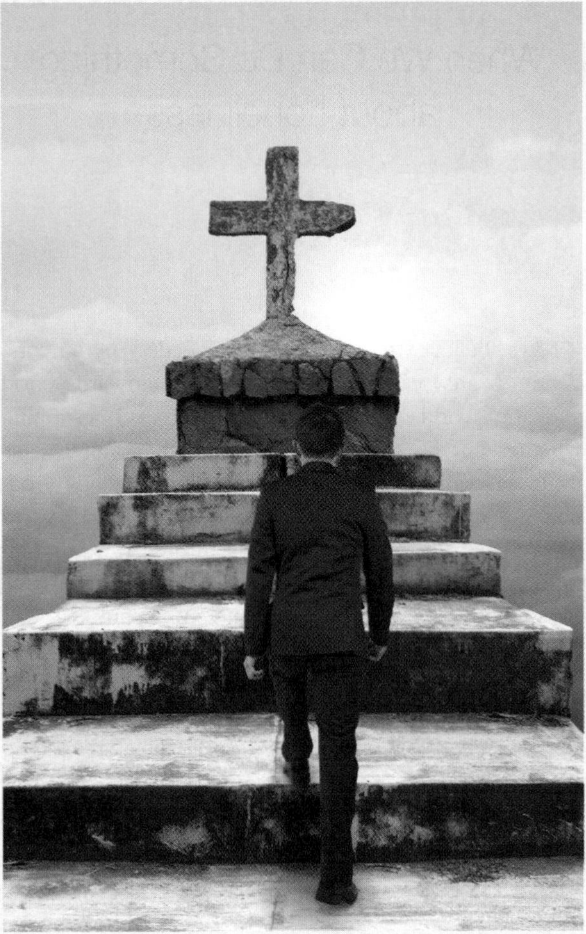

The joy of the gospel fills the hearts and lives of all who encounter Jesus. Those who accept his offer of salvation are set free from sin, sorrow, inner emptiness, and loneliness. With Christ joy is constantly born anew (Pope Francis, *Evangelii Gaudium*, 2013).

Changing Bitterness to Acceptance

In Christ's Crucifixion, we find that God has made himself our companion in suffering. When we humbly seek him from the deepest part of our pain, we find that in the very act of looking for him our hearts begin to change as we hear him saying "truly, I say to you, today you will be with me in Paradise." These are the words spoken to one of those crucified beside him. This man did not demand an explanation from the Saviour. Accepting his death sentence, he simply asked Jesus to remember him in his Kingdom (*Lk* 23:43b). There was also a second man hanging beside Jesus. He could not accept the status quo. He probably thought "how is it possible for Jesus to claim that he is the Saviour, hanging next to me, defeated?" He mocked Jesus. We too may find, like this man, the idea of searching for God in our pain laughable. "After all," we might argue, "if God truly cared about me, he would take me out of this horrible mess!" In this state of mind, our hearts may be screaming insults at God since he appears to remain indifferent to our pain. In our disappointment, we might demand that God should "do something!" (cf. *Lk* 23:39). These two ways of dealing with chronic loneliness – acceptance and denial – point to our need to hear the truth. If our hearts have hardened against God, it is because we have believed the perennial lie of the Devil: that God cannot be trusted (*2 Co* 11:3). But the Good News is that God has done something about our pain! When the world was convinced that the Saviour had been defeated, Jesus arose from the dead! His resurrection silences the lying voice of Satan that tells us that he is more powerful than God in our lives. In Jesus, the Cross is not the end, but it has become the way to finding God. That way begins with the call to faith and true repentance (cf. *CCC* 2608).

Trusting God in Loneliness

Repentance does not mean simply feeling bad about ourselves. Instead, it is the beginning of trust. It is an act of faith that believes, even just a little bit, that God is not indifferent to our burden, and that he wants us to find him. We may ask, "well why doesn't God simply show himself to me?" The answer to this question is that he already has – it is just that we may not agree with the way he has done it. When Jesus was brought before Pontius Pilate to have him judged as a criminal deserving the death sentence, Pilate presented Jesus back to the people telling them to judge Jesus instead. The raging mob judged Jesus to be an imposter, not a

Saviour King but a weak man. They condemned Jesus as being incapable of giving them what they really wanted – freedom from Roman oppression. They wanted a better life, no taxes and so on. Instead of Jesus, they asked for the rebel Barabbas to be released. They bayed for Jesus's blood. They cried out "crucify him!" (cf. *Mt* 27:26). Similarly, when Jesus appears to us today, he does not always appear as we would necessarily like him to be – perhaps we want him to be a sort of superman who will solve all our problems. At the end of time Jesus will appear in all his Glory and power to establish his Kingdom once and for all, but for now we discover him in his poverty. He was poor from the cradle to the Cross (cf. *Mt* 25:31). Perhaps some of us are feeling so much pain right now that when we speak about searching for God, we just want to shut our ears and burst in on the silence of the stable in Bethlehem. We want to shake the manger where the baby Jesus is laying, and demand from him to "do something" about our problem. But he does do something. His response to our anger is his cry of helplessness (cf. *Lk* 2:7). And now, on the Cross, his hands and feet bound, we still demand that Jesus should "do something!", but there he remains silent until he cries his words of absolution for our unjust condemnation. What we really mean when we wave our fists at God is that he should change our circumstances to the way that we want them to be. It means that we have no faith to believe that God knows what is best for our salvation. God's power is in his silence. God's strength is in our weakness (cf. *2 Co* 12:9). We are called to trust God in our pain. Trust is an act of faith. It is a response to his invitation to go "beyond what we feel and understand" (*CCC* 2609). God the Father sent his only Son Jesus Christ not to make our lives a bit better, but to reconcile us with the Father for Eternal Life. We are never alone if we allow Jesus Christ to be our companion and guide. He willingly shares our burden (*Mt* 11:29), but at the same time, he shows us how to pass through the valley of the shadow of death to hope (cf. *Ps* 23:4-6).

Letting Go of Disappointments

If our hearts are heavy with disappointment towards God, the Gospel provides us with the way to be free – it is the way of repentance and faith. The Good News proclaims that "God so loved the world that he gave his only Son, that whoever believes in him should not perish but have eternal life" (*Jn* 3:16). As Christ was being crucified on Golgotha, only those who were not disappointed with him experienced the power of his love because they accepted his weakness as the source of his authority. God speaks most profoundly to our hearts when we receive his total gift of himself as the Crucified Saviour without expecting something else. By not letting go of our disappointments in loneliness, we prevent ourselves from identifying with the suffering and death of Jesus. Acceptance allows us to trust God and to cry out "Lord, remember me when you go beyond death!" (cf. *Lk* 23:42). When we are unable to reconcile with our loneliness, and when we reject the world that we feel has denied us, we find that no amount of company will ever truly satisfy us. Only the Holy Spirit can really guide us towards sincere repentance. He makes us discern the direction in which our hearts need to turn (cf. *CCC* 2847). When our situation of loneliness is caused by circumstances beyond our control, we are called to acceptance – to suffer with Christ on the Cross. When we discover that our loneliness is caused by our pride, we must act. We may find that we have isolated ourselves from others because they have disappointed us, and we have taken offence. As husbands and wives, we may be lonely because we cannot tolerate our spouses as they are, and so we demand that they change to suit us. As brothers and sisters, we may be holding on to judgements against each other, or we may have turned our backs on our parents because we cannot forgive them for the way they treated us. Our friends can easily disappoint us too. When we choose to keep silent rather than have it out with them we can end up losing contact with many of them over the years. In all these and similar situations, we may find ourselves alone because we have given in to disappointment. We may have allowed our hearts to harden towards others because we carry their offences.

"Why should we forgive?" is an excellent question to ask. Forgiveness is always difficult when we see it as a matter of letting somebody off the hook. When we carry with us unforgiveness, we carry with us the debt that others owe us. Our emotional demands for payment can soon add up. Some of us carry around the equivalent of entire filing cabinets of demands for repayment. The heaven of communion that God wants to offer us does not permit excess baggage. When Jesus uttered the words "Father forgive them" on the Cross, he was deliberately letting go of everything that would prevent him from rising again (cf. *Lk* 23:34). In his prayer of the Our Father, Jesus teaches us to be bold in asking God for forgiveness. We experience communion to the extent that we are free to receive it. When we do not let go of our emotional demands for justice, there is no space in our hearts to gain the power that sets us free to enter into communion with others. We can forgive in Jesus because the forgiveness that is pronounced in his name is a fruit of the resurrection. In choosing to allow ourselves to forgive in the name of Jesus Christ our relationships are renewed in a way that would not have been possible without his power.

Turning Loneliness into an Adventure

St Augustine famously described our search for God as restlessness; our hearts are restless until they rest in God (cf. *CCC* 30). The Bible presents us with the history of

God's intervention in the life of a people leading up to the coming of Jesus as the Saviour. Abraham is an important person for us to know in our search for God. He was an old man without children. He and his wife, Sarah, were perceived as social failures in their day because of it. Not having descendants meant that they could not live on through their children. However, God intervened in their history by revealing himself to them, and promising that Abraham would be the father of nations if he would follow the Lord as his God. It meant that Abraham had to set out on a journey of faith to receive the promised gift of a son. After disappointments and setbacks, he eventually received a son whom he named Isaac, born to his elderly wife, Sarah. By leading Abraham on a long adventure through a dialogue of prayer and obedience, God led him to grow in faith (cf. *Gn* 12:1-21:7). If like Abraham, we begin a journey to find God in our loneliness, we will have to accept that we do not know where we are going or how we are going to get there. We are called to trust that through our obedience to God he will not disappoint us (cf. *CCC* 145). The Catechism describes faith as "the assurance of things hoped for, the conviction of things not seen" (*CCC* 146). It describes the obedience of faith as hearing and freely submitting to God's word which is "Truth itself" (*CCC* 144). The way we respond to loneliness can determine how we understand ourselves. We can see ourselves as either victims or the protagonists in the story of our lives.

Pope John Paul II speaks about his journey towards the priesthood in his autobiographical book *Gift and Mystery* where he interprets the events of his life with the eyes of faith. Born in Wadowice, Poland and baptised Karol Józef Wojtyła, the time of the Second World War was particularly difficult and lonely for him, since all that was familiar to him was taken away by the occupying Nazi forces. His father died during that time from a heart attack when he was twenty years old. He had already suffered the death of his mother when he was nine, and his elder brother when he was twelve. But despite all of this he looked back at his life with gratitude, seeing all the events as part of a rich adventure that led to his priesthood. He could easily have looked back with bitterness. Our response to loneliness is determined by our trust in God as a loving Father who does not abandon his children. For this reason, the Church calls us to take courage. The life of Joseph, in the Old Testament, illustrates this point. He was the favourite son of Jacob. Out of jealousy, his eleven brothers sold him into slavery. He ended up as the slave of Potiphar in Egypt. He was treated well until Potiphar's wife tried to seduce him unsuccessfully. Out of spite she falsely accused Joseph of assaulting her and had him thrown into prison. There, when he was most alone, and everything seemed lost, it was discovered by the Pharaoh that God had given Joseph the gift of interpreting dreams. Since the Pharaoh had experienced a particularly disturbing dream, he asked Joseph to help him. Because of this, Joseph was instrumental in saving the nation from famine. He was then freed and awarded the position of the Prime Minister of Egypt. His dramatic change of fortune meant that he was eventually able to welcome his eleven brothers and their father to settle with him in the oasis of Egypt (cf. *Gn* 37:12-42:38). Looking back at his life, Joseph could very easily have identified himself as a victim and taken revenge on his brothers. Instead, he chose to accept that it was God who had guided the events of his life. When it comes to our experience of loneliness, there may be nothing that we can do to change our situation physically. We may find ourselves, like Joseph, alone and imprisoned when we have to face occasions such as sickness, losing our job, bereavement, homelessness and so on. Like Joseph, we can take courage and choose not to identify ourselves as victims, but to trust that God is leading us on an adventure towards a treasure.

Prayer

O Lord, I am sorry for the times I have rebelled against your goodness when I have felt so lonely. Please give me the gift of true repentance and faith. I thank you for not turning away from me in those dark moments. Please fill me with the consolation that comes from your Holy Spirit so that I may find my place with all the saints in your Kingdom.

Tips for Finding God in Loneliness

- When trying to discern if God is calling you to accept your situation of loneliness or to change it remember the well-known Serenity Prayer. "God, grant me the serenity to accept the things I cannot change, the courage to change the things I can, and wisdom to know the difference" (attributed to Reinhold Niebuhr).

- Ask your parish priest how you can be more involved in the life of the parish.

- Find opportunities to do kind things for others without looking for any reward. For example, find out if your local hospital has a group that visits patients who are lonely and offer your services.

- In times of temptation towards bitterness, meditate on Jesus's call to discipleship. "Then Jesus told his disciples, 'If any man would come after me, let him deny himself and take up his cross and follow me'" (*Mt* 16:24).

Praying in Loneliness

Every religion shows that we all have a desire for the God who made us. In our loneliness, it is natural for us to search for God. However, we can only know him when he reveals himself to us. We discover him to be a loving God. In the Bible, we see that God always takes the initiative in calling us to him. From Abraham to Jacob, Moses, King David and Elijah the prophet, God gradually prepared humanity to receive his Son, the promised resolution to the Devil's envy. Even though we may not always be in tune with his call, God never fails to give each of us individually the necessary help that we need to find him. Ever since the fall of our first parents, God has been working to allow us to connect with him once again and to know his love for us. God wants nothing more than for us to 'walk' with him (cf. *Gn* 5:24). In the Bible, Jesus promises us that his Heavenly Father will give good things to those who persist in asking, seeking and knocking on his door (cf. *Mt* 7:7-11). The Church interprets this incessant search as prayer. If we pray very little, we can find ourselves going nowhere in God's plan for our lives; the less we pray, the less we want to pray. In our loneliness, we may be tempted to abandon prayer altogether. However, when we do give up on it, we may end up finally losing any trace of trust that we had in God. Prayer must go beyond our feelings and even our understanding. It must depend on our faith. At critical moments on our faith journey, God gives us the graces we need to pray regularly. If we do not exercise that grace, through our conversion of heart, we lose it. We may then find it harder to pray until the very idea of spending time with God becomes meaningless. A vacuum is then left in our spiritual lives that needs to be filled; invariably we will fill it by sinning. In this case, we need to overcome our difficulties in prayer by humbling our hearts, trusting that God will come to help us and by not giving up. Jesus has opened a way to the Father so that we can unite our loneliness with the will of God and obtain from him the courage to accept it. The surest way to a life of prayer is to work towards keeping a rhythm of prayer throughout the day, for example, first thing in the morning and in the early evening. Two particular devotions can help us to grow in our relationship with the Lord: Eucharistic Adoration and the Holy Rosary.

Eucharistic Devotion is an Antidote for Loneliness

When Jesus and his disciples celebrated the Last Supper, they were doing what the Jews had always done.

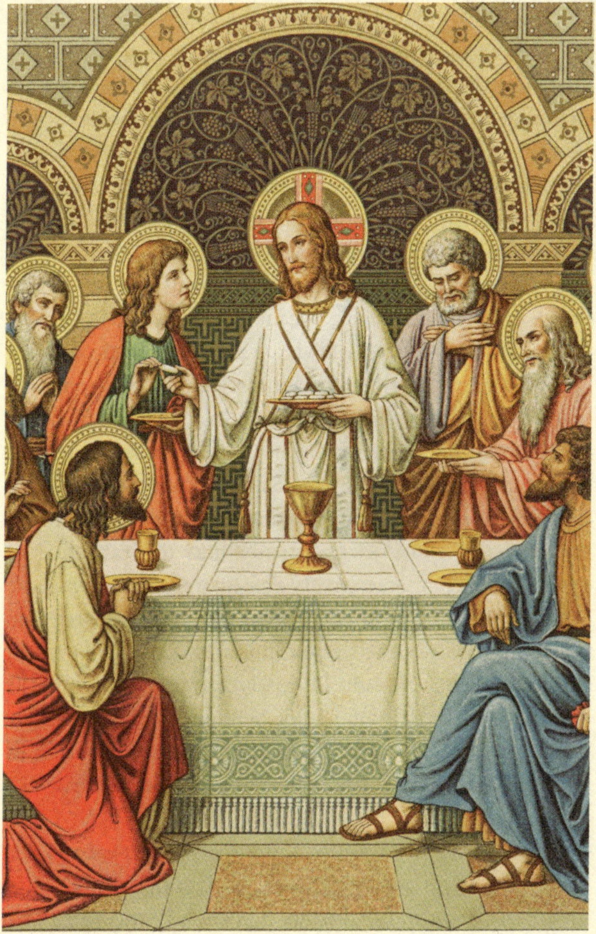

They were remembering the events leading up to the liberation of God's chosen people from slavery in Egypt. However, Jesus now identified himself as the new Passover Sacrifice. His blood was to be poured out on the Cross to liberate his people from the slavery of sin (cf. *Ex* 12:7). Every time we celebrate the Holy Mass, the Blessed Sacrament of the Eucharist makes Christ's Passover present to us. He 'passed-over' from death to life. In the Holy Eucharist we are not alone because Christ's Body, Blood, Soul and Divinity are made truly present to us by the power of the Holy Spirit and by the words of consecration spoken by the priest (cf. *CCC* 1358ff). By celebrating the memorial of Christ's Passover, we are not simply being nostalgic – calling to mind past events, like an ancient story that is told and retold – but allowing ourselves to come sacramentally into the presence of God himself. For Israel, every Passover makes present the same power of God that led their forefathers to freedom (cf. *CCC* 1363). Now, the memorial of Christ's Sacrifice, offered over two-thousand years ago, is made sacramentally present to us whenever we celebrate the Mass. It is also described as the "sacred banquet of communion with the Lord's body and blood" (*CCC* 1382), by which we are brought to intimate union with Christ and our baptised brothers and sisters who share in the Eucharist. By receiving Christ sacramentally through Holy Communion, we also receive the same risen Christ who died for our sins. Simply by being in his sacramental presence, we can experience his power to save us from the temptations that accompany loneliness. By his Cross, he has "disarmed the principalities and powers and made a public example of them, triumphing over them" (*Col* 2:15). There is a moment within the Mass which calls us to gaze upon the Holy Eucharist and to behold Jesus truly present. "The Eucharistic presence of Christ begins at the moment of the consecration" (*CCC* 1377-1378). At this important moment the priest celebrating the Mass holds up and presents the Body and Blood of Jesus for the assembly to adore. In Eucharistic Adoration this moment is extended outside of the Mass when the Sacred Host is presented on the altar in a Monstrance for veneration. Adoration can also be done before a tabernacle in a church or chapel. By regularly praying before the Blessed Sacrament we can develop a deeper and more consoling relationship with the Lord in our loneliness. Fr Raniero Cantalamessa, the preacher to the papal household, proposes that adoring Jesus in the Blessed Sacrament is a way of companionship. He tells us that by contemplating Christ in the Eucharist in silent prayer we receive the Trinitarian gift of God himself who loves to be with us.

> [There is the experience of] a heart-to-heart contact with Jesus really present in the Host and, through him, of raising oneself to the Father in the Holy Spirit…

Sometimes Eucharistic contemplation just means keeping Jesus company, being there under his gaze, giving him the joy of contemplating us, too. (Raniero Cantalamessa, *The Eucharist, Our Sanctification*, 1995)

Holy Hour

How should we pray in the presence of the Blessed Sacrament? Fr Cantalamessa points to St Jean-Marie Vianney (1786-1859), a priest from Ars, in France. After witnessing a peasant praying simply before the Blessed Sacrament without words, he described adoration as a two-way relationship, where we look at Jesus in the Host and allow him to look back at us (ibid.). Just as with anyone we love, we do not need lots of words to be in the presence of the Lord. Another French priest, St Peter Julian Eymard (1811-1868), proposed that we spend our time before the Blessed Sacrament with four ends in mind. Named by Pope John Paul II as "Apostle of the Eucharist", from an early age, he had a great love for Eucharistic Adoration and would often be found near the Tabernacle where the Sacred Hosts are kept. He was canonised by Pope John XXIII during the close of the first session of the Vatican II Council in 1962. During his priestly ministry, he founded the Congregation of the Blessed Sacrament where members would commit themselves to Eucharistic Adoration for twenty-four hours a day. In his catechesis on Devotion to the Blessed Sacrament, he encouraged adorers to divide their time of adoration to follow the four ends of the Holy Sacrifice: to adore Jesus, to thank him, to be sorry for sins and to ask him for good things. St Eymard encourages us, before leaving our time of adoration, to make a resolution that we should be mindful of the Lord during the day and to resolve to make "some sacrifice" that we will offer him that day. By also keeping in mind these four aspects of the Holy Eucharist – adoration, thanksgiving, repentance and intercession – we can be helped to participate more fully in the Holy Mass and so enter a more profound communion with both the Lord and our worshipping community (St Peter Julian Eymard, *How to Get More out of Holy Communion*).

The Rosary Announces the Good News

There is a close link between the Word of God, the Eucharist and the Rosary. The Rosary has been a productive devotion in the life of the Church as an antidote to loneliness. It is a contemplative prayer which connects us with our brothers and sisters across the whole Church since our meditation of the Gospel Mysteries is founded on the words of the Our Father, joining us together as God's children. It is important to recognise when praying the Rosary that it is a meditative prayer based on the Good News that Satan has been defeated. At its heart is the Incarnation – the Word was made Flesh through the obedience of Mary and dwelt amongst us (cf. *Mt* 1:23). When we pray the Rosary, we relive the Mysteries as a memorial of the mighty intervention of God in the life of his people. In the Jewish understanding of 'memorial,' it is a case of remembering – that is a 'putting-back-together-again'. For the Jews, the Passover is a reliving of the time that God's mighty hand freed his people from Egypt. In this sense, it is possible to see how the power of God is made present to us through the prayerful recitation of the Rosary. It is a contemplative prayer that, if prayed with faith and devotion, can lead us to a deeper intimacy with the Lord and a greater understanding of his plan for our lives. It is a prayer especially recommended for those who are caught up in the pangs of loneliness and are searching for God. Praying the Rosary every day can save us from the oppression of doubts and the destructive forces of evil. By regularly substituting our time with the television, the internet or any other distractions with the recitation of the Rosary we begin to experience the power of the Gospel opening up to us. We can pray all four Mysteries together if we have the time or just pray one of the Mysteries on any given day.

Pope John Paul II tells us in his Apostolic Letter on the Rosary, *Rosarium Virginis Mariae,* that he attributed the many graces he received in his life to this prayer. He tells us that by meditating on the Mysteries we share in Mary's contemplation. Significantly, we are not just looking back, but we make those events present to us now. For the Jews, this understanding of remembering the events of the Exodus from the past as a way of making them present today is at the centre of their annual Passover Celebration. The Hebrew word for this kind of remembrance is *zakar*. Similarly, our recollection with Mary of the events that took place in the Gospel makes present to us the same grace that operated in those events. This means that we should pray with faith, expecting that the Lord's Word has power. We think of the promise of Jesus that entire mountains can be thrown into the sea if we pray with faith (*Mk* 11:22-23) or the woman who was healed of her bleeding because of her faith after touching his garment (*Mk* 5:24-34). We too should not doubt but believe that the Lord has the power to cast the "mountains" and problems of our lives into the abyss and that he can heal our wounds when we open ourselves up to the power of the Gospel in the Rosary. Pope John Paul II tells us:

> These events not only belong to "yesterday"; they are also part of the "today" of salvation. This making present comes about above all in the Liturgy: what God accomplished centuries ago did not only affect the direct witnesses of those events; it continues to affect people in every age with its gift of grace. To some extent this is also true of every other devout approach to those events: to "remember" them in

a spirit of faith and love is to be open to the grace which Christ won for us by the mysteries of his life, death and resurrection. (Pope John Paul II, *Rosarium Virginis Mariae*, 2002)

By praying the Rosary with faith, therefore, we can allow the power of the Good News to penetrate our deepest experience of loneliness. It is fundamentally a meditation on the Gospel, following the Joyful, Luminous, Sorrowful and Glorious Mysteries of the life of Jesus. With each Mystery, there are five events that we call to mind over the course of ten Hail Mary prayers. We recite the Our Father at the start of each decade and conclude each one with the Glory Be. We do not rush the words of the prayer but allow them to blend with the images of the Gospel that we are pondering. A set of Rosary beads can help prevent us losing count of our prayers, but fingers and thumbs can suffice if we do not have one. The Rosary is a really simple prayer; however, if you are unsure about how to pray it, it is a good idea to ask someone who has the experience to go over it with you. There are also lots of good devotional books which explain how to pray the Rosary in a lot more detail, for example, *A Simple Rosary Book* by the Catholic Truth Society. Through our humble prayers and devotions, we can find a way through our loneliness and receive the graces that we need to find the God who loves us.

Prayer

Heavenly Father, I want to know you, but I see that I can easily give up in my search for you. Thank you for the love you have shown to me by coming to find me. Please give me the grace of humility and perseverance in prayer so that I may come to accept your will in my life.

Tips for Finding God in Loneliness

- Why not make a personal Holy Hour each week by visiting a church or chapel where the Blessed Sacrament is reserved? Resolve to spend time regularly in prayer before the Blessed Sacrament. Find out from your diocesan office where there is a church that has Eucharistic Adoration on a regular basis.

- Make a habit of meditating on the Rosary daily. Take time to contemplate each of the Mysteries, keeping in mind the power of the Word to make present to your life the grace of each Mystery.

- Meditate on Jesus's promise: "he who eats my flesh and drinks my blood has eternal life, and I will raise him up at the last day" (*Jn* 6:54).

Prayers

St Thérèse of Lisieux (1873-1897) describes prayer as a "surge of the heart; it is a simple look turned toward heaven, it is a cry of recognition and of love, embracing both trial and joy." It is described by the Church as raising the mind and heart to God and asking God for good things (cf. *CCC* 2558-2559). Here is a very brief selection of prayers which can be used to help in times of loneliness.

Anima Christi

Soul of Christ, sanctify me
Body of Christ, save me
Blood of Christ, inebriate me
Water from Christ's side, wash me
Passion of Christ, strengthen me
O good Jesus, hear me
Within Thy wounds hide me
Suffer me not to be separated from Thee
From the malicious enemy defend me
In the hour of my death call me
And bid me come unto Thee
That I may praise Thee with Thy saints
and with Thy angels
Forever and ever. Amen.

Guardian Angel Prayer

Angel of God, my Guardian dear, to whom God's love commits me here, ever this day (or night) be at my side, to light and guard, to rule and guide. Amen.

Who Will Help Me?
Hildegard of Bingen (1098-1179)

Where am I? How did I get here? Whom can I ask to comfort me? How will I break these chains of sin that enslave me? Whose eye can bear to look at these ugly spiritual wounds that disfigure me? Whose hands will anoint me with oil that I may be healed? Who will help me unless it is you, O God? Whenever I think of the glorious freedom which you promise, my slavery to sin seems ever more oppressive. Whenever I think of the beauty of your Son, my spiritual ugliness seems even more terrible. Whenever I think of the joyful music of your love, my soul sinks into despair. Dear God, what will become of me?

O Lord My God
St Anselm (1033-1109)

O Lord, my God, teach my heart this day where and how to find you. You have made me and remade me, and you have bestowed on me all the good things I possess, and still, I do not know you. I have not yet done that for which I was made. Teach me to seek you, for I cannot seek you unless you teach me, or find you unless you show yourself to me. Let me seek you in my desire; let me desire you in my seeking. Let me find you by loving you; let me love you when I find you. Amen.

For Seekers of Faith

St Benedict (480-547)

Gracious and holy Father, give us the wisdom to discover you, the intelligence to understand you, the diligence to seek after you, the patience to wait for you, eyes to behold you, a heart to meditate upon you, and a life to proclaim you, through the power of the spirit of Jesus, our Lord. Amen.

Spiritual Communion

O Jesus, I firmly believe that you are truly present in the Blessed Sacrament. I see you full of love, willing to pardon us, anxious to be united with us. I wish most earnestly to respond to your desire and love. I detest all the sins by which I have ever displeased you. Pardon me, O Lord! I desire to receive you into my heart, and since I now cannot receive you sacramentally, come at least spiritually to me. I embrace you, I unite myself with you as if you were really present in my heart. With all my love I cling to you. Preserve me from sin, that I may never be separated from you, but remain united with you forever. Amen.

Four Ends of Eucharistic Adoration
After St Peter Julian Eymard (1811-1868)

Try to find a Catholic church where you can sit before the Tabernacle uninterrupted for a set period of time. Praying the Rosary or simply sitting in silence is a good thing to do. As a suggestion, you might find it helpful to divide your time of prayer into four sections in adoration, thanksgiving, repentance and intercession. For example, half an hour divided into four seven and a half minutes, or one hour divided into four fifteen minutes. Each of the four segments does not have to be equal in time. A prayer is suggested here after each heading, but you are encouraged to also pray in your own words. Do not be afraid to keep periods of silence too:

1. **Adoring Jesus.** *"Lord Jesus, I adore you and praise you for your Mercy towards me. I praise you for your majesty and glory…"* etc.

2. **Thanking Jesus.** *"Lord Jesus, together with all of the Saints in heaven and the Holy Virgin Mary, I thank you for loving me with the gift of your body, blood, soul and divinity…"* etc.

3. **Repentance.** *"I take responsibility and repent of all my sins and I choose you Jesus, to be my Lord and Saviour…"* etc.

4. **To ask whatever you will.** *"Lord Jesus, I ask of you for the following special favours…"* etc.

Useful Resources in the UK

Catholic Resources:

The Catholic Bishops' Conference of England and Wales Providing information about the Catholic Church in England and Wales. *(www.cbcew.org.uk)*

The Dympna Centre A Catholic counselling service for clergy and religious. Phone: 01423 817515. Postal address: Parkside House, 17 East Parade, Harrogate, HG1 5LF. *(www.thedympnacentre.co.uk)*

The Retrouvaille Program For married couples facing difficult challenges in their relationship. Phone: +1 (800) 4702230. *(www.helpourmarriage.org)*

Cor et Lumen Christi Community A Eucharistic-centred community that seeks to build a spiritual extended family in which all the vocational states of life are at home. Phone: 0741 9375213 Mon, Wed, Thu, Fri; 11:00-13:00, 14:00-17:00. Write: Highfield House, St John's Way, Chertsey, Surrey KT16 8BZ. Email: corlumenchristi@gmail.com *(www.coretlumenchristi.org)*

Youth 2000 Young people leading young people into a life-transforming relationship with Jesus Christ. Offering young adults retreats, missions and leadership formation. Write: Youth 2000, Pilgrim Bureau, Friday Market Place, Walsingham, Norfolk NR22 6EG. Phone: 01328 821153 – 07585 039442. Email: info@youth2000.org *(www.youth2000.org)*

Mental Health Project A mental health project set up by the Catholic Bishops' Conference of England and Wales. Postal address: Catholic Bishops' Conference of England and Wales, 39 Eccleston Square, London. SW1V 1BX. Phone: 020 7901 4826. *(www.catholicmentalhealthproject.org.uk)*

Universalis This is a free-to-use online resource containing the prayers of the Divine Office and the daily Mass readings. *(www.universalis.com)*

Non-Catholic Resources:

Samaritans A UK charity that offers a safe and confidential 24-hour listening ear for any problems. Phone: 116 123. Email: jo@samaritans.org Write: Freepost RSRB-KKBY-CYJK, PO Box 9090, STIRLING, FK8 2SA *(www.samaritans.org)*

The Together Project A British community interest company, tackling age segregation in care homes by arranging for mothers and toddlers to attend care homes to share activities with elderly residents on a regular basis. *(www.thetogetherproject.co.uk)*

Pet Bereavement and Pet Loss Support for those grieving for the loss of a pet, whether through death, parting or enforced separation. Phone: 0800 0966606 from 8.30am to 8.30pm. *(www.bluecross.org.uk/pet-bereavement-and-pet-loss)*

Association of Christian Counsellors A professional body set up in 1992 to facilitate quality counselling, psychotherapy, pastoral care and related training. *(www.acc-uk.org)*

Alcoholics Anonymous A charity that offers fellowship to men and women in finding hope and help to recover from alcoholism. Phone: 0845 769 7555. *(www.alcoholics-anonymous.org.uk)*

Emotions Anonymous Following the 12 Step program of recovery. The website is based in the US and provides information on where meetings are held around the world, including the UK. *(www.emotionsanonymous.org)*

Suggested Reading:

de Montfort, Louis and Barbour, Mary (trans.). *The Secret of the Rosary*. (New York, TAN Books, 1993)

Larrañaga, Ignacio. *Sensing Your Hidden Presence: Towards Intimacy with God*. (New York, Doubleday, 1987)

Lozano, Neal. *Unbound: A Practical Guide to Deliverance* (Ada, Michigan, Chosen Books, 2003)

Bibliography

Cantalamessa, Raniero. *The Eucharist, Our Sanctification*. (Collegeville, Minnesota, The Liturgical Press, 1995)

Catechism of the Catholic Church: the CTS Definitive & Complete Edition. (London, Catholic Truth Society, 2016)

Eymard, Peter Julian. *How to Get More out of Holy Communion*. (Manchester, New Hampshire, Sophia Institute Press, 2000)

Francis. *An Apostolic Exhortation issued 'Motu Proprio.' Evangelii Gaudium*. (London, CTS, 2013, Print)

Francis. *Address to Participants in the International Colloquium*. Synod Hall, Monday, 17 November 2014

John Paul II. *Meaning of Man's Original Solitude*. General Audience of 10 October 1979

John Paul II. *Gift and Mystery: On the Fiftieth Anniversary of my Priestly Ordination*. (New York, Doubleday, 1996)

John Paul II. *Apostolic Letter, Rosarium Virginis Mariae*. (London, CTS, 2002, Print)

Paul VI. *Presbyterorum Ordinis*. 1965